The Legend of the Wraggi Haggis Wars

~

Tony Kerfoot

With illustrations by Terry Adams

This book is dedicated to my wife Linda. My rock in all storms.

On the stone of telling,

Beyond each tiny dwelling,

An ancient sage sits and speaks,

Of magic past and war unique.

And there upon the telling stone,

As if upon a royal throne,

A legend there is slowly born,

Amid the fields of barley corn,

With battle tales none can ignore,

From the Wraggi Haggis war!

The legend begins...

Of Wraggi folk in ancient times,

Oft told were simple nursery rhymes,

Of how they fought the Haggis hordes,

With bristling fur and sharp-edged swords,

As snouts held high, they took their stand,

Against each wild marauding band.

They say the battles fiercely raged,

Through ambushes most carefully staged,

By Wraggi chiefs who did their best,

To lay the Haggis hordes at rest,

As mounted on great highland hares,

They charged forth to raucous cheers.

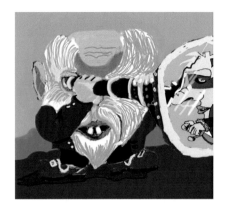

As blades flashing left to right,

They put the Haggis folk to flight,

From Campbeltown to Inverness,

From north and south to east and west.

With steely cries of "Quick advance!",

The Wraggi fought at every chance,

Fur a-quiver, snouts upraised,

Through every glen a path they blazed.

"The moors are ours!" they shouted loud,

And common Wraggi snouts, once bowed,

Were lifted high with obvious pride,

Saluting now the victory side.

And, with each new Haggis rout,

The battles slowly faded out,

Until at last, a peace descended,

As the Wraggi Haggis wars were ended.

Then, by lochs and hillside glens,

Brave warriors linked snouts with friends.

As tired soldiers laid down arms,

To hurry home to moorland farms,

Where, in burrows deep beneath the heather,

Wraggi mums and bairns together,

Waited in eager anticipation,

For the celebratory invitations.

Finally through the doors they came,

Gold embossed with heroes names.

"We're sure you will find it a real delight,
Please attend our Wraggi night."
No-one from the feast was banned,
Aged Wraggi limped along,
To join the others in a song,
As work began in earnest,
To ensure all drinking urns were burnished
Never had so much been done,
Nor with such tremendous fun.

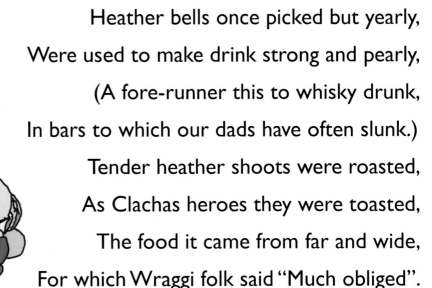

Heather bells once picked but yearly,
Were used to make drink strong and pearly,
(A fore-runner this to whisky drunk,
In bars to which our dads have often slunk.)
Tender heather shoots were roasted,
As Clachas heroes they were toasted,
The food it came from far and wide,
For which Wraggi folk said "Much obliged".

Buzzing bees came in a hurry,
With honey sweet to fill each tummy.
The grouse brought gifts of crystal water
(Gertrude simply brought her daughter).
The hares supplied the fur for chairs,
White ducks flew by in haughty pairs,
Mice and others of their kind,
Simply brought what they could find.

Excitement ran at fever pitch,

And Wraggi snouts began to twitch,

As they caught the scent of cooking smells,

That drifted out past the wells.

Throughout it all, elder Wraggi sagely sat,

(With tartan bonnets on their laps),

And talked about the olden days,

When Wraggi folk had different ways,

While fur was patted, primped and preened,

And leather sporrans carefully cleaned.

The little ones that couldn't sleep,

Were firmly left in Grandma's keep,

And every minute on the hour,

Young female Wraggi took a shower.

Revenge of the Haggis...

But even as the Wraggi played,

Their enemy watched from deepest shade,

And filled with blood-lust for revenge,

Began to plot the Wraggi's end,

And so it was the Haggis ran,

To talk to devious Pictish Man!

At dead of night all dressed in black,
In shadowy bar and woodland shack,
Evil schemes were nightly made,
As Man and Haggis pledged their aid.
"We have a common aim," they said,
"To see the awesome Wraggi dead!"

No wonder then at dubious meets,
They talked of dark, horrid feats,
And treachery stalked the land,
As heated passions, they were fanned,
By memories of great humiliation,
Blamed upon the poor Wraggi nation.

The Haggis talked of night attacks,
(Though oft their leaders lacked the facts),
To mount a proper war campaign,
That guaranteed a battle gain.

Then one Haggis, more bold than most,

Stood up and proposed a toast.

"I've spoken to the Tigh-Na-Ran,

Who've given us the perfect plan,

A wizard friend of theirs, they say,

Will help us all to win the day."

The clamour ceased as each in turn,

Hushed to listen and to learn,

Just how and when and where,

The Wraggi they'd make disappear.

Then as the words were spoken out,

The loathsome crew began to shout,

"A spell, a spell!" they cried with glee,

"Few Wraggi from that will easily flee!"

And so it was, in the wee small hours,

Before the sun warmed heather flowers,

That groups of stealthy Haggis raiders,

Crossed the borders of their neighbours,

Until, beneath leafy boughs,

The Haggis stood, disguised as owls.

And there, beneath each Wraggi burrow,

The smell of owls caused brows to furrow.

For, of all those that Wraggi fear,

The owl is clearly premiere!

But, being filled with food and drink,

(With snouts lit-up and in the pink),

The Wraggi appeared unconcerned,

(A mistake, they sadly learned),

For as the feasting reached its peak,

The Haggis their revenge did wreak!

As from the flasks of spells prepared,

Death they loosed in burrows aired,

And chroniclers say the Haggis did succeed,

In this their final evil deed...

Sadly then this tale we tell,

Of how at last the Wraggi fell.

But still their name it lingers on,

In childhood dream and childhood song,

But even there our story cannot end,

For what of the Haggis, my dear friend?

In very short time they dearly paid,

For treating the Wraggi in such cruel ways.

For while they danced to highland reels,

Having cast aside great wooden shields,

Men were planning a double-cross,

That would see the Haggis totally lost.

And so before pale dawn broke through,

The Haggis began to reap their due.

The Haggis get their comeuppance...

As doors, un-creaking were stealthily locked,

Leaving all escape routes firmly blocked,

Before tipsy revellers saw their plight,

And rushed headlong into flight.

And finally when the Haggis woke,

It was as captives 'neath Man's harsh yoke,

And soon they tilled Man's ground,

Completely shackled, chained and bound,

Nor was it easy to complain,

While working hard 'neath snow and rain,

For labouring under watchful eyes,

They quickly found that time it flies.

And so, eventually with fur all worn,

And clothes that hung in tatters torn,

Were found the Haggis in pitiful state,

Finally accepting their cruel fate.

"Oh why, oh why?" they daily cried,

"Were we so keen to keep our pride?

Though beaten by the Wraggi clans,

We never suffered at their hands!"

At this Man laughed loud and long,

And said, "With the Wraggi dead and gone,

We stand unchallenged on this, our land –

Something from the first we planned!"

And burdened by deep-seated guilt,

Sad Haggis hearts began to wilt.

But then another set of cards were dealt,

To worsen how the Haggis felt,

When after years of cruel abuse,

Man fell upon yet another ruse,

When they invited to dinner dates,

The Haggis whom they served on plates.

In other words they got their comeuppance,

Being sold in butchers, just for tuppence!

Which explains why now, in modern day,

At Burns' night suppers Man often pays,

Tribute to this Chieftan o' the Puddin Race,

While eating them with ill-hid grace!

And so were the Haggis legends born,

A product of Man's deep-seated scorn.

Survival...

Now, come on, let's be fair,

Our story shouldn't just end there.

So if while walking heather moors,

Perchance you've time to stop and pause,

You might, by some strange quirk of light,

Catch a glimpse of pink eyes bright,

Or see in some earthen groat,

What looks to be a pinken snout!

If so, then you too can say,

"Perhaps a Wraggi I saw today!"

Beware though should the eyes be red,

Or if your heart be filled with dread,

As you watch the creature standing quiet and still,

Upon some dark and craggy hill,

It may well be a Haggis dreaming of revenge,

That's quietly stalking you dear friends!

First though let's think on brighter things,

Like August grouse that flee on wings,

As wild as the highlands they portray,

On warm and blue-sky'd sunny days.

And should you hear faint song nearby,

It may well be a Wraggi shy,

Prepared to vanish in a puff,

Should your voice seem over gruff.

Furry wee balls of pink and brown,

That ever scamper on moorland grounds,

Ploughing the funny little furrows,

That lead to well-hid Wraggi burrows.

And if a Wraggi you should meet, be sure,

Not to shut your memories door,

Or let the magic moment pass,

But rather pray that it will last,

For in myth's vast imagination,

We've never known a gentler nation.

So, when in Scotland next we walk,

Or over moors and through glens you stalk,

Keep the Wraggi well in mind,

Doing nought to jeopardise their kind.

Equally, keep a watch for highland fowls,

Least you meet the Haggis – disguised as

OWLS!

Acknowledgments

For Zoe, Jonny, Megan, Christopher and Peter.

And to my grandchildren: Alistair, Kathryn, Daniel, Erica, Sophie, Lucy, and Sebastian, and any others to come. May you all flourish.

I would also like to thank Terry Adams for illustrating the text, turning a dream into reality.

Thanks too Zoe, Bill and Barbara, who pushed me to get it done.

ISBN: 978-0-9927468-2-7

Published in 2014 with the assistance of Lumphanan Press